Extreme
Weather

This edition published in 2009 by
The Five Mile Press Pty Ltd
1 Centre Road, Scoresby
Victoria 3179 Australia
Website: www.fivemile.com.au
Email: publishing@fivemile.com.au

Conceived and produced by Weldon Owen Pty Ltd
59-61 Victoria Street, McMahons Point
Sydney, NSW 2060, Australia

Copyright © 2008 Weldon Owen Pty Ltd
First printed 2009

WELDON OWEN GROUP
Chairman John Owen

WELDON OWEN PTY LTD
Chief Executive Officer Sheena Coupe
Creative Director Sue Burk
Concept Development John Bull, The Book Design Company
Art Manager Trucie Henderson
Senior Vice President, International Sales Stuart Laurence
Vice President, Sales: United States and Canada Amy Kaneko
Vice President, Sales: Asia and Latin America Dawn Low
Administration Manager, International Sales Kristine Ravn
Production Manager Todd Rechner
Production Coordinators Lisa Conway, Mike Crowton

Senior Editor Barbara Sheppard
Designer John Bull/The Book Design Company
Illustrators Christer Eriksson, Dr Mark Garlick, Andy@KJA-studios, MBA Studios,
Dave Tracey, Guy Troughton

ISBN: 978-1-74211-431-6

Colour reproduction by Chroma Graphics (Overseas) Pte Ltd
Printed by SNP Leefung Printers Ltd
Manufactured in China

10 9 8 7 6 5 4 3 2 1

A WELDON OWEN PRODUCTION

▶in*siders*

Extreme Weather

H. Michael Mogil and
Barbara G. Levine

The Five Mile Press

Contents

introducing

What Is Weather?

Weather Goes Wild

Observing Weather

in *focus*

introducing

Weather Engine
The Sun

Every place on Earth has weather and climate. Weather is the state of the atmosphere above Earth. It includes wind, clouds, storms, temperature, humidity and precipitation, such as rain and snow. Climate is the average of weather conditions over a period of years. Both weather and climate are fuelled by the Sun, which gives off energy in the form of solar radiation, mostly visible light. Only about half the energy coming from the Sun is absorbed by Earth's surface and converted into heat. The other half is either reflected back into space or absorbed by the atmosphere. Near the Equator, the Sun's rays strike Earth directly and much of the Sun's heat is absorbed. Near the North and South poles, however, the Sun's rays are more slanted and less heat is absorbed.

Global patterns
At any given time there are many weather events happening around the world. Lines of storms and low-pressure systems are affected by high-altitude and surface winds. Ocean currents move warm and cold water around the globe and help equalise temperatures between the poles and the Equator. Man-made pollution, forest fire smoke, ash from volcanoes and dust particles all contribute to Earth's weather.

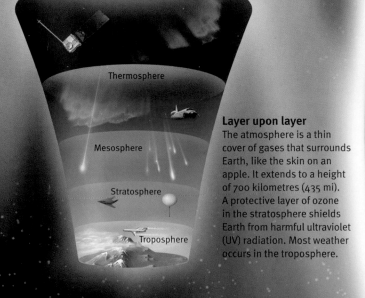

Layer upon layer
The atmosphere is a thin cover of gases that surrounds Earth, like the skin on an apple. It extends to a height of 700 kilometres (435 mi). A protective layer of ozone in the stratosphere shields Earth from harmful ultraviolet (UV) radiation. Most weather occurs in the troposphere.

Exosphere

Thermosphere

Mesosphere

Stratosphere

Troposphere

Solar heat *The Sun's rays warm Earth's surface. Land temperatures change more than those in the water. Bright white snow can reflect 90 per cent of the Sun's energy, while dark green rainforests absorb a large amount of energy.*

Ocean storm *Outside the tropics, intersecting warm and cold fronts create massive storm systems. Often much larger than hurricanes, they rarely contain hurricane-force winds.*

Hurricane *Intense, rotating storms that form over warm water near the Equator are known as hurricanes in the Atlantic Ocean. These storms are called typhoons in Asia and cyclones near Australia and India.*

Fast-moving air *The jet stream is a narrow band of high-speed winds found 8–20 kilometres (5–12 mi) above sea level.*

On fire *Large amounts of smoke and ash rise into the atmosphere when forests burn. Airborne pollutants like these can act like a cloud and block sunlight.*

Sandstorm *Strong surface winds, often produced by desert thunderstorms, can easily pick up dust and sand. Several times a year, dust from Africa travels all the way across the Atlantic Ocean to North America.*

CHANGING SEASONS

Because Earth's axis is tilted 23.5 degrees, varying amounts of sunlight reach the Northern and Southern hemispheres during the year. When a hemisphere is tilted towards the Sun, it is summer there. When a hemisphere is tilted away from the Sun, it is winter.

Northern spring, southern autumn

Northern summer, southern winter

Sun

Northern winter, southern summer

Northern autumn, southern spring

Change in Pressure

Wind

Wind is air in motion. Winds blow at all levels in the atmosphere and every place on Earth. Changes in air pressure and temperature usually start and maintain winds. As warm air rises, the number of air molecules at ground level is reduced, forming an area of low pressure. As air cools, it sinks and increases the number of air molecules, forming an area of high pressure. Air then moves from the high-pressure area to the low-pressure area, creating wind. The greater the pressure difference between the two areas, the stronger the wind. Small pressure changes result in light breezes, while large ones can make hurricane-force winds.

Blown around

Wind can create waves on bodies of water and push water onto low-lying areas. Coastal regions are prone to strong winds because cooler air over the water blows onshore to replace rising warm air. As wind speed increases and decreases, creating gusts, trees sway and sometimes break.

Crashing surf *As a wave approaches the shoreline, the bottom of the wave is slowed by friction while the top continues to move forwards and crests. Strong winds push water inland.*

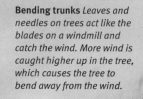

Bending trunks *Leaves and needles on trees act like the blades on a windmill and catch the wind. More wind is caught higher up in the tree, which causes the tree to bend away from the wind.*

Coriolis force *As Earth rotates, global winds are deflected between high- and low-pressure areas. Winds bend to the right in the Northern Hemisphere and to the left in the Southern Hemisphere.*

Hadley cell

Ferrel cell

Polar cell

Equator

Wind patterns *Major global winds blow from the east near the poles and the Equator and from the west in the middle latitudes. Circulating areas, or cells, of rising and falling air wrap around Earth.*

LOCAL WINDS

Small temperature variations between nearby surroundings can cause local wind patterns. Winds always blow from cooler to warmer places. Local winds occur near coasts, in mountainous regions and between urban and suburban areas.

Cool air over sea

Warm air over land

Land and sea breezes During the day, cooler air from over the water rushes onshore to replace rising warm air. Overnight the process reverses.

Valley winds As slopes are heated by the Sun, the warm air rises. This air eventually cools and falls. At night, warm air above cools and flows down mountain slopes, creating a cool wind.

Flying debris *Pieces of buildings and branches blown at high speeds can become dangerous, even deadly, missiles.*

Water in the Air
Clouds

Clouds are masses of condensed water vapour that collect around tiny particles, such as dust, in the air. Most clouds form as warm air rises, then expands and cools. Clouds are also made by weather fronts; when air is forced up mountain slopes; and when sunlight heats the ground, causing air to rise. Puffy cumulus clouds develop when rising air currents are intense. Layered stratus clouds form when updraughts are gentle. Fog is a stratus cloud that touches the ground. Clouds look white because water droplets reflect and scatter sunlight. Dense clouds appear dark because light cannot pass through.

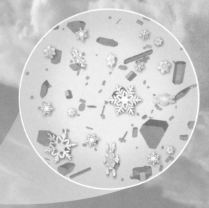

Frozen water
Wispy cirrus clouds contain ice crystals. In freezing cold air, water vapour changes directly to ice or snow. The shape of the snowflakes depends on the temperature of the air, water vapour and ice crystals within the cloud.

Threatening storm
Large, dark clouds and strong winds signal an approaching storm. Squall lines that contain many intense thunderstorms form along a band of low pressure. They can regenerate with new thunderstorms, which form ahead of the rain curtain. Squall lines may last for six hours or longer.

Lined up *Altocumulus are puffy clouds in a layer. They are often aligned in rows or bands. Altocumulus clouds form from gently rising air or they may remain after a thunderstorm dissipates.*

Showers *It doesn't rain everywhere underneath clouds. Raindrops can be suspended by rising air. Precipitation generally occurs with sinking air. Downdraughts are visible as grey curtains of rain.*

WATER CYCLE

Water continually evaporates, forms clouds, falls as precipitation and collects in rivers, lakes and seas. The cycle shapes Earth's weather and provides a continuous supply of fresh water.

Clouds build up over land

Rainwater collects in lakes and rivers

Clouds form

Water flows to the sea

Water evaporates

Rain *Air movement in a cloud collides microscopic water droplets and merges them together. Millions of water droplets are needed to make one drop of rain. If the raindrops grow large enough, they fall to Earth.*

Leading edge *Shelf clouds, usually with flat bases and puffy tops, mark the front of a thunderstorm. Cold, outflowing winds force air outside the cloud to rise and can generate new thunderstorms.*

Whitecaps *Wind blowing across the water's surface causes ripples and waves to form. Winds stronger than 65 kilometres per hour (40 mph) make the surface appear frothy.*

Supercell
Thunderstorms

Approximately 40,000 thunderstorms form around the world each day, with 2,000 occurring at any one time. Thunderstorms develop when warm, moist, unstable air rises to high altitudes. They begin to die out almost as soon as they form, when cool downdraughts outnumber warm updraughts and rob the cloud of energy. Typical thunderstorms last 1–2 hours and all have bursts of lightning and thunder. Supercell thunderstorms, one of the most severe kinds of weather on Earth, last much longer and may produce torrential rain, damaging hail and tornadoes. Intense downdraughts of air, called downbursts, may strike the ground with winds that sometimes exceed hurricane force and can knock an aeroplane out of the sky.

Violent cloud

Most thunderstorms have a three-phase life cycle, which may take only a few minutes or last several hours. They form during the day when sunlight heats the ground or when rising air interacts with mountains and weather fronts. The bottom of a towering cumulonimbus, or thunderstorm, cloud can be a thousand metres off the ground.

Tall tower *The top of a thunderstorm may reach the tropopause. Powerful updraughts can push the upper limit above 18,000 metres (60,000 ft), more than twice the height of Mt Everest.*

Dying out The cumulonimbus cloud disintegrates as cool downdraughts cut off the storm's supply of rising air. Often only a patch of wispy cirrus clouds remain behind.

Surface damage Tornadoes, intense swirling winds, can descend from a supercell thunderstorm. When tornadoes touch ground, their damage is easy to see. Sometimes, one home is destroyed, while others nearby are unharmed.

carry water vapour upwards into cooler air. The moisture condenses, forming puffy cumulus clouds.

Whirling Winds
Tornadoes

Tornadoes are violent, spinning winds that reach speeds of more than 300 kilometres per hour (185 mph). Rotating winds inside an intense thunderstorm concentrate water vapour into a tight vortex. The distinctively shaped funnel that descends from the storm's wall cloud rarely lasts longer than 10 minutes. Supercell thunderstorms can produce tornadoes that wreak havoc for more than an hour. Long-lived tornadoes tend to be very wide, sometimes 1.6 kilometres (1 mi) across, and kill the most people. Extensive damage occurs where wind speeds change significantly and along the paths of small tornadoes inside the main funnel. Central United States is called "Tornado Alley" since hundreds of tornadoes occur there each year, the most for such a small area anywhere in the world.

Heavy lifting *The force of tornado winds, the strongest on Earth, can carry massive objects for several kilometres. These winds are able to lift cars, train carriages and entire houses.*

Destructive force

Tornadoes do not cause houses to explode. Roofs are ripped off by fierce winds. Airborne wreckage, such as tree limbs and vehicles, can impale buildings, shatter windows and cause devastating structural damage.

Anatomy of a tornado
Tornadoes are created by rotating winds inside a big thunderstorm and spiralling ground winds. Debris clouds provide evidence that a tornado has reached the ground.

Thunderstorm

Wall cloud

Funnel

Ground wind

Debris cloud

Hollow tube *Low air pressure inside the funnel cloud creates a calm core surrounded by powerful, twisting winds. From the outside, tornadoes can look like snaking ropes, cones or elephant trunks.*

Flash in the Sky
Lightning

Lightning is the visible part of a giant, atmospheric electric spark. It is the result of a buildup of opposing electrical charges inside a towering thundercloud. The temperature of lightning can reach 30,000°C (54,000°F), five times hotter than the Sun's surface. The intense heat causes air to expand at supersonic speed and produce a clap of thunder. Scientists estimate that 3 million lightning flashes happen daily around the world. Lightning strikes thousands of people each year and most survive. It is said that "lightning does not strike the same place twice," but annually the Empire State Building in New York City is struck approximately 100 times.

Dangerous discharge

Lightning usually strikes the highest point, such as an isolated tree, tall building or sometimes even a person out in the open. When threatening thunderstorm clouds are close, head for shelter inside a building or enclosed car. A lightning flash can ignite forest fires, destroy electronic equipment and stop a heartbeat.

HOW LIGHTNING FORMS

Most lightning occurs in cumulonimbus clouds that contain violent air currents. Negative charges accumulate near a cloud's base. Positive charges are lifted by updraughts and the ground beneath the storm can become positively charged.

Cloud-to-ground If there is a positive charge on the ground, lightning may strike downwards from the cloud.

Cloud-to-cloud Lightning can jump within one cloud or between opposite charges in nearby clouds.

Cloud-to-air Electricity may travel from positive charges inside the cloud to surrounding negatively charged air.

Sound system *Lightning is seen almost immediately, but thunder travels much more slowly. To find out how far away a storm is, count the delay between the flash and the thunder. A three-second interval represents a distance of 1 kilometre (0.6 mi).*

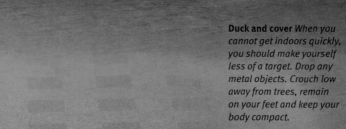

Duck and cover *When you cannot get indoors quickly, you should make yourself less of a target. Drop any metal objects. Crouch low away from trees, remain on your feet and keep your body compact.*

Branching out *Lightning travels in erratic paths towards oppositely charged particles. Flashes can look like broad arcs, bent forks or small streamers that extend upwards from the ground or the top of a tree.*

Back and forth *At almost the same time lightning leaves the cloud, a return path reaches up from Earth. Electricity moves rapidly between the charged areas a few times. Lightning can strike 8 kilometres (5 mi) away from a thunderstorm.*

Up in flames *Searing heat from a lightning strike can boil sap and explode a tree. Fiery flying embers may cause houses, dry grasses or other trees to catch fire.*

Grounded *Lightning may run along the surface or penetrate deep into the soil. The flow of electricity helps to re-establish the balance of charges.*

Cyclones, Typhoons and
Hurricanes

A hurricane is an intense, spiralling storm that can measure up to 800 kilometres (500 mi) across and produce torrential rain and inland flooding caused by a storm surge. Hurricanes are often referred to as "the greatest storms on Earth" and may contain winds up to 300 kilometres per hour (190 mph). They can last for days, or even weeks, and have a long, destructive history of sinking ships and devastating coastal areas. Hurricanes form over tropical water, usually in summer. These storm systems are known as typhoons near Asia and cyclones near Australia and the Indian Ocean.

Strengthening storm

Most hurricanes that affect Europe and the US start as a cluster of storms off the African coast. As the storm moves away from the Equator, it strengthens and starts to spin. The storm may intensify and weaken many times as it moves across the ocean. The hurricane will slow down when it reaches land.

Stage 2 *Clouds organise into spiral arms as rotation and wind speed increase. The storm system is called a tropical storm when it has sustained winds between 63–118 kilometres per hour (39–73 mph).*

Stage 1 *Hurricanes begin as a group of thunderstorms located near the Equator. High-altitude winds bring the storm clouds together and start them spinning. The storm system is fuelled by warm, moist, rising air.*

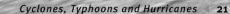

Path of destruction

Powerful hurricane-force winds and the accompanying storm surge can flatten buildings, lift entire houses, and flip cars and boats. Many people die in hurricanes every year when they cannot get to safe shelter.

Updraughts *Warm, rising air feeds towering storm clouds. Bands of dense rainfall concentrate below the storm's spiral arms.*

Eye wall

Eye

Stage 3 *When wind speeds exceed 118 kilometres per hour (73 mph), the storm system is called a hurricane. The calmest region in a hurricane is its centre, or eye. The strongest winds are in the eye wall, the area that surrounds the eye.*

Coastal flooding *Persistent, strong winds can create a storm surge that pushes sea water several kilometres inland. Pounding waves cause destructive beach erosion. Hurricanes weaken and die out as they move over land or cold water.*

Storm at Sea

Wall of Water

Many low-pressure weather systems involve interactions between cold, dry continental air masses and warm, humid oceanic air masses. As these air masses meet, storm systems with cold and warm fronts develop. In the middle and high latitudes, these low-pressure storms can intensify quickly: they are often several times larger than tropical storms and winds may reach Category 1 hurricane strength. When wind patterns and surface water temperatures produce the right conditions, fierce winds can create devastating waves.

View from space
This satellite photograph shows a huge, mid-latitude storm, with typical Northern Hemisphere anticlockwise spiralling winds raging over the British Isles. Because of the Coriolis force, storms in the Southern Hemisphere rotate clockwise.

Boat *It is nearly impossible for a boat to navigate huge, reinforced waves. To survive, captains try to point the vessel into the path of the oncoming wave. If broadsided, the boat would most likely capsize.*

Combined effect *Wind-generated ocean waves can reinforce each other to build taller, stronger waves. Some interfere with other waves, lessening the overall height. Waves only crest in open water if winds are strong enough to push the top over.*

Dangerous ocean

The crew of a fishing trawler is trying to keep their boat afloat as a monstrous wave approaches. Intense ocean storms with hurricane-force winds can form when a tropical storm collides with a low-pressure system. Winds from the resulting storm may generate 30-metre (100-ft) ocean waves. In comparison, the largest tsunami—a wave that is caused by an earthquake, landslide or volcanic blast—measured 524 metres (1,720 ft).

OCEAN CURRENTS

The major ocean currents are created by global wind patterns. They carry warm water (red arrows) and cool water (blue arrows) long distances and can strongly influence weather. For example, the Gulf Stream current, which transports warm water from the Caribbean Sea to the North Atlantic Ocean, makes the climate of northwestern Europe milder than it would be otherwise.

Washed Away
Floods

Floods are responsible for 40 per cent of all deaths from natural disasters. They can be caused by heavy rainfall; dam, levee and ice jam breaks; and coastal storm surges. Widespread heavy rains can make rivers break their banks. Large-scale river flooding can last longer than a month, ruining houses and destroying farmland. Paved roads and other hard surfaces decrease rain absorption and increase runoff. Barriers built to keep water out, such as dams and levees, can give a false sense of security. If these structures collapse suddenly, the result can be disastrous.

Raging water

Flash floods happen when too much rain falls too quickly. A downpour in the mountains may create flash flood conditions under clear skies several kilometres away. Water channelled through steep canyon walls is strong enough to move cars, houses and boulders. It will wipe out everything in its path. There is no way to outrun such a flood. Luckily, two hikers have escaped the floodwater and climbed to safety.

Increased risk *Sun-baked riverbeds and dry ground act like pavement. Water runs off instead of being absorbed.*

High above *In mountainous areas, narrow canyons collect rain quickly. A canyon can act like a funnel, concentrating and speeding up the flow of water as it crashes downhill.*

Water power *Flash floods can travel 16 kilometres per hour (10 mph). The force of water moving at this speed is equivalent to winds in a strong Category 1 hurricane.*

FLOOD PROTECTION

Areas at risk of flooding can be protected by strong barriers built to hold or restrict floodwater. But protective structures in one location may raise water levels in a nearby place without safety measures.

Levee Reinforced earthen walls contain rivers that change course often or overflow regularly.

Tidal barrier In low-lying coastal regions, barriers stop abnormally large waves and control tidewater.

Dam A dam is a concrete wall that blocks or regulates the flow of a flood-prone river.

Coping with
Extreme Heat

Heatwaves kill more people than all other forms of extreme weather. These extended periods of higher-than-average temperature can last from a couple of days to several weeks. Heatwaves become deadlier when daytime heat soars and night-time temperatures remain high. In Europe in 2003, a 10-day heatwave was responsible for an estimated 35,000 deaths. A record high temperature in Seville, Spain, reached 47.2°C (117°F). Silent killers, without obvious damage and destruction, heatwaves most severely affect the elderly, young or ill. Drought conditions, when a below-average amount of rain falls, often happen at the same time as heatwaves.

Oasis *Layers of rock beneath the desert trap water. Plant roots that reach down into the underground reservoir draw on the water to survive. People use pipes to transport water up to the surface.*

Lack of rain

Deserts are dry regions that receive little rain. They cover one-seventh of Earth's land surface. Nomadic peoples in the Sahara Desert often use camels as pack animals because they can survive with little water. Deserts are not always hot. Antarctica is the world's driest continent and less than 25 cm (10 in) of precipitation falls on that vast, frozen desert each year.

Blowing sand *Wind speeds greater than 16 kilometres per hour (10 mph) bounce and pick up sand grains. Airborne sand moves at about half the wind's speed. Strong winds and rising air currents can transport dust halfway around the world.*

ANIMAL ADAPTATIONS

To survive in the desert, animals need to withstand temperature extremes and find, save and recycle water. Some produce nearly dry droppings so minimal moisture is lost. Many species hunt for food only at night to avoid overheating.

Heat transfer Blood vessels near the surface of a jackrabbit's large ears release excess body heat efficiently.

Wet bag A burrowing frog covers itself in a sack of moist, discarded skin to prevent drying out. The frog can remain underground in this hibernation-like state for years, or until it rains again.

Ships of the desert *Camels can go for many days without drinking because they have the ability to retain water. Their hump stores food, and woolly fur keeps them cool. Their body allows them to "heat up" but not perspire.*

Optical illusion *A mirage is a shimmering air mass that looks like a puddle. It forms when distant light is bent, or refracted, as it passes through a layer of hot air near the ground that sits below cooler air.*

Proper attire *Loose clothes allow air to circulate and trap moisture to prevent dehydration. A head cloth shields the face and neck from scorching heat and the sting of airborne sand.*

Auroras

When particles in the solar wind collide with Earth's atmosphere they vibrate. As they return to their original state, they give off different colours of light. Oxygen particles release red, green and yellow light. Auroras, most common around the polar regions, occur 80–600 kilometres (50–370 mi) above Earth's surface.

The Sun is the source of all weather in our Solar System. Gases blow from the Sun's thin atmosphere in a constant wind of magnetically charged particles. This solar wind travels through space and takes 2–6 days to reach Earth. A magnetic field surrounding Earth protects the planet from the solar wind's harmful effects, such as communication disruptions, and diverts the charged particles towards the North and South poles. If they reach Earth's atmosphere, the particles can cause magnetic storms but also produce auroras, beautiful light shows in the night sky. In 1989, a solar storm lasting 9 hours created magnetic currents so strong that Quebec's power grid shut down. The power failure affected 6 million electric customers in Canada and the US.

Lights in the sky
Weather in space includes colourful displays of light called aurora borealis, or "northern lights", and the Southern Hemisphere equivalent, aurora australis. Seen from Earth, auroras resemble bright glowing streamers and curtains.

PLANETARY STORMS

Solar energy makes weather on all planets in our Solar System. Bitterly cold Mars has large daily temperature variations, ice caps made of carbon dioxide and dust devils. Lightning may flash from clouds in the carbon-dioxide-filled atmosphere above Venus.

Flames of gas Solar flares happen when energy erupts from the Sun's surface and blows holes through the star's thin atmosphere.

Jupiter's Great Red Spot This violent storm, twice the size of Earth, has been raging on Jupiter like a giant hurricane for more than 300 years.

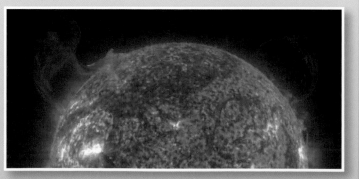

Inside the
Eye of a Storm

Meteorologists—scientists who study weather—have developed sophisticated techniques and machines to monitor and record weather conditions and help them make increasingly accurate forecasts. Observation equipment is placed at weather stations around the world: at the poles, in deserts, in the oceans and on satellites in space. Most data is transmitted electronically and gathered by computers. The information is checked for accuracy and processed into weather maps, charts and written reports. To collect information about hurricanes and severe storms, scientists rely on Doppler radar and storm spotters and fly piloted and unmanned planes directly into a storm.

Hurricane hunter

Special aircraft fly through the clouds over a storm around 12,000 metres (40,000 ft) above sea level. Onboard instruments, such as radar, measure conditions in the storm. Orbiting satellites, buoys, ships and coastal observation stations provide extra data.

Down the hole *Hurricanes have an almost clear, well-defined eye. Although not perfectly still, the eye is calm compared to the surrounding eye wall, which has the strongest winds.*

Eye wall

Falling probe *Scientists release an equipment-filled canister, called a dropsonde, into the eye. It measures wind, temperature, pressure and humidity every half second on the way down. Slowed by a parachute, it takes about 15 minutes to reach the sea below the hurricane.*

U.S. AIR FORCE

Spinning clouds *Spiral arms contain stronger winds and heavier rains than the calmer regions between the bands. The storm's coiling structure is reinforced by inwardly spinning low-level winds.*

Bumpy ride *Hurricane hunter aeroplanes are designed to handle the turbulence inside a storm. Meteorologists buckle up for safety and securely fasten all equipment.*

WEATHER DETECTION DEVICES

About 300–400 years ago, inventors like Galileo, Torricelli, Fahrenheit and Celsius developed some of the first instruments to record weather data. Their equipment is still used today, along with radar, satellites and computers.

Rain gauge
The amount of rain that falls in 24 hours is collected in a tube.

Thermometer
Temperature is measured with a thermometer.

Barometer
Air pressure is tracked with a barometer.

Anemometer Wind speed is measured by how quickly the cups spin around.

Weather balloon
Equipment attached to balloons monitors Earth's atmosphere.

Ocean buoy Floating equipment platforms collect data about air and water conditions.

Changing
Climate

Earth was formed 4.6 billion years ago and its temperature has increased and decreased through history. At times it has been warmer than it is today, and sometimes much colder. Weather conditions have changed dramatically in recent years, in part due to increased carbon dioxide emissions and human activities. In the last 100 years, Earth's average temperature has risen about 0.6°C (1°F); carbon dioxide levels in the atmosphere have increased 33 per cent; and the amount of ice cover has decreased significantly. Carbon dioxide traps heat inside Earth's atmosphere, much like how the windows of a greenhouse keep warm air inside. Some scientists suggest that the rise in temperature, referred to as "global warming", will make Earth's weather more extreme.

Crack in the wall *As melting occurs on the top of an ice sheet, water pools and seeps into crevices. This weakens the structure of the ice and increases the rate of calving.*

Temperature over time
Since the 1800s, when people started burning coal in factories to produce power, carbon dioxide emissions have increased and so has Earth's average temperature (marked by the red line).

Global average temperature

	°C	°F
	16.0	60.8
Mean temperature		
	15.0	59.0
	14.0	57.2

1900 1925 1950 1975 2000
Year

Falling ice

Antarctica's ice sheet, the world's largest glacier, contains about 90 per cent of all the ice on Earth. When a chunk of ice breaks off, or calves, it is carried by ocean currents to a warmer climate where it melts. Meltwater contributes to rising sea levels, which can alter ocean currents and cause flooding.

Tip of the iceberg *Large pieces of freshwater ice that calve from ice sheets are known as icebergs. Only 10 per cent of an iceberg floats above the water's surface.*

Breaking free *Melting and calving ice removes mass from an ice sheet. Each year, snowfall adds back some of the mass. Overall, ice sheets are shrinking because new snow is not keeping up with the loss of ice.*

RECEDING GLACIER

Glaciers around the world are shrinking at a rapid pace as temperatures rise and snowfall levels change. These photos, taken in 2002 and 2003, show how far Switzerland's Triftgletscher Glacier retreated in a single year.

2002

2003

WIND

NEW ORLEANS, HURRICANE KATRINA: THE FACTS

STORM LOCATION: **New Orleans, Louisiana, USA**

STORM DATE: **23–30 August 2005**

STORM STRENGTH: **Category 5 over Gulf of Mexico; Category 3 at landfall**

DEATH TOLL: **1,833**

Fast facts Fast facts at your fingertips give you essential information on each event being explored.

Locator map This map shows you where the featured event occurred. Look for the red area on each map.

WATER

Side bar This side bar indicates what kind of extreme weather event is being examined.

HEAT

in *focus*

WIND

Gobi Desert
Dust Storm

The right combination of fierce winds and prolonged dry weather can produce massive dust storms and sandstorms. All deserts and many areas where vegetation is sparse are vulnerable. Dust particles are about one-tenth the size of sand grains, so dust remains airborne longer and is carried further than sand. Dust may travel thousands of kilometres and rise up 3,000 metres (10,000 ft) into the atmosphere. Some dust storms are so extensive that they are visible from space. Airborne dust and chemicals cause health problems and damage fragile coral reefs. Drastically reduced visibility and clogged engines affect train and aeroplane transportation.

GOBI DESERT, DUST STORM: THE FACTS

STORM LOCATION:	Gobi Desert, China
STORM DATE:	9–11 April 2006
STORM STRENGTH:	No commonly accepted scale
DEATH TOLL:	9

Dust fills the sky
A massive dust storm engulfs a village in Gansu Province, near the Gobi Desert. Such storms occur often in northwestern China where poor land management, sandy topsoil and the encroaching desert have caused widespread erosion and desertification. In 2006, nine dust storms hit the region in a two-month period. Sometimes, the dust reaches Japan, Korea and even the US.

WATER

HEAT

Approaching cloud *Dust storms can travel as fast as 80 kilometres per hour (50 mph). Near the origin, these storms may arrive with almost no warning. Occasionally, precipitation dropping through a dust cloud creates falling mud.*

Piled up *These storms can deposit thousands of tonnes of dust and sand. Sand drifts, caused by strong winds, can bury homes, farm equipment, crops and roads.*

Dusty blanket
A towering wall of dust brought by a strong cold front covered Melbourne, Australia, in 1983. After the storm passed, the city had to remove an estimated 1,000 tonnes of dust.

Traffic hazard

Airborne dust mixed with pollution created an eerie haze over Beijing, China, in 2001. Skies can appear yellow, red, brown or black depending on the type and thickness of the dust.

Stopping erosion *Farmers place bundles of straw in the ground as barriers against windblown sand. The Chinese government has set up a programme to plant trees and shrubs as windbreaks.*

Storm tracks
Each coloured mark shows the position of a tornado touchdown. Some of the tornadoes remained on the ground 16–32 kilometres (10–20 mi) or longer.

EF4
EF3
EF2
EF1
EF0

Tennessee
Double Trouble

TENNESSEE, DOUBLE TROUBLE: THE FACTS

STORM LOCATION: Jackson, Tennessee, USA

STORM DATE: 5 February 2008

STORM STRENGTH: EF4 and EF3 tornadoes

DEATH TOLL: 0

In a 24-hour period, lasting from 12 p.m. on 5 February 2008 until 12 p.m. the next day, an estimated 133 tornadoes ploughed across an eight-state region in the US. The tornadoes were concentrated in Tennessee, Kentucky, Arkansas, Alabama and Mississippi. It was the second-highest 24-hour tornado total ever recorded. Unseasonably warm temperatures fuelled the supercell thunderstorms that spawned most of the tornadoes. This devastating outbreak occurred several months before the regular tornado season and, unusually, many of the deadly storms formed at night. Across the eight states, 84 people died. One tornado carried an 11-month-old boy for about 90 metres (300 ft). Incredibly, he survived with only minor injuries.

Blown apart
The two twisters that hit Union University in Tennessee damaged 80 per cent of the dormitories. The stronger tornado, with wind speeds more than 265 kilometres per hour (165 mph), was rated EF4 on the Enhanced Fujita Scale. The second funnel to rip through the university was an EF3 tornado. Several students were trapped in rubble but nobody died on campus died.

Paired up *Tornadoes do not always form alone. Sometimes, one or more funnels rotate around a central tornado. Multi-vortex tornadoes, originating from the same cloud, create unpredictable damage patterns. One building may remain untouched, while around it, everything is flattened.*

WIND

WATER

HEAT

Myanmar
Cyclone Nargis

Packing winds up to 195 kilometres per hour (120 mph), Cyclone Nargis became one of Asia's deadliest storms. The Category 3 cyclone made landfall on the low-lying Irrawaddy Delta of southern Myanmar (formerly known as Burma). Nearly 85,000 people died because of the storm's intensity, flood-prone location and lack of adequate warning systems. Hundreds of thousands of farm animals were also killed. Cyclone Nargis was the first storm of the region's summer monsoon season. Although the word "monsoon" is often used to refer to torrential rains, it actually means a seasonal change in winds. Much of Southeast Asia and India experience both wet and dry monsoon periods.

MYANMAR, CYCLONE NARGIS: THE FACTS

STORM LOCATION: Irrawaddy Delta, Myanmar

STORM DATE: 2–3 May 2008

STORM STRENGTH: Category 3

DEATH TOLL: Approximately 85,000

Advancing floodwaters

Relentless winds forced a 3.5 metre (12 ft) storm surge up to 40 kilometres (25 mi) inland. The only escape was to climb to safety. Many people remained in trees for days until the raging floodwaters receded.

Storm surge *A shallow patch of water precedes the storm surge. The push of wind-driven waves onto coasts only a metre or so above sea level does not allow water to drain back to the ocean.*

Flooded fields
The salty storm surge devastated the delta's highly productive agricultural region. Mangrove trees, a natural defence against flooding, had been cut down so the land could be farmed.

Ripped apart *Although some houses are raised as protection from occasional high tides, large waves and fierce winds knock down walls and undermine a building's entire structure.*

WIND

WATER

HEAT

New Orleans
Katrina

Hurricane Katrina was the costliest hurricane, and one of the five deadliest, to ever strike the US. The hurricane was responsible for 1,833 deaths and several hundred people are still listed as missing. Coastal areas were devastated from Florida to Texas. The storm was a highly destructive Category 5 hurricane over the Gulf of Mexico, but it had weakened to Category 3 by the time it made landfall near New Orleans on 29 August 2005. New Orleans is below sea level, located between the Mississippi River and a large lake. The city's protective levees failed during the storm, causing catastrophic flooding. People were unable to return to their homes for many weeks. Hurricane Katrina was one of 27 named storms during 2005, the greatest number in a single hurricane season.

NEW ORLEANS, HURRICANE KATRINA: THE FACTS

STORM LOCATION: New Orleans, Louisiana, USA

STORM DATE: 23–30 August 2005

STORM STRENGTH: Category 5 over Gulf of Mexico; Category 3 at landfall

DEATH TOLL: 1,833

Sunken city

For days after Hurricane Katrina, people were stranded in flooded neighbourhoods. Muddy water, contaminated by hazardous materials and waste, submerged cars and property. Houses were ruined by floodwater and the growth of mould and mildew.

Floating help *Trapped inside buildings by rising water, people broke through roofs to escape. More than 11,000 people were rescued by boats.*

Levee failure *Hurricane Katrina's strong winds pushed high waves and a 7–8.5 metre (24–28 ft) storm surge inland 10 kilometres (6 mi). The force of the water eroded the banks and broke levees, flooding 80 per cent of the city.*

Airlift *The US Coast Guard used more than 40 helicopters for rescue missions. They pulled 12,000 people to safety.*

WIND

Peru
Mudslide

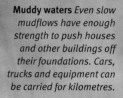

PERU, MUDSLIDE: THE FACTS

STORM LOCATION: Chanchamayo, Peru

STORM DATE: 22 January 2007

STORM STRENGTH: No commonly accepted scale

DEATH TOLL: 16

Rainwater flowing down mountains and narrow canyons can move with enough force to undercut roads, knock down trees and destroy homes. Warning signs of an imminent mudslide include suddenly rising stream levels, buckling streets and visible gaps appearing in walls. Every two to seven years, a weather pattern called El Niño brings unusually warm ocean currents and heavy rain to the west coast of South America. During that time, less rain falls on the other side of the Pacific Ocean in Australia and Indonesia, often resulting in drought. El Niño cycles last between one to two years. They alternate with La Niña cycles that bring warm water to the western Pacific Ocean. El Niño and La Niña affect weather around the world. Torrential rain fell in Peru from December 2006 to January 2007 during an El Niño cycle.

Muddy waters *Even slow mudflows have enough strength to push houses and other buildings off their foundations. Cars, trucks and equipment can be carried for kilometres.*

WATER

EL NIÑO AND LA NIÑA

Changes in water temperature in the Pacific Ocean create El Niño and La Niña weather patterns. In the maps below, warm water is shown in red and cool water is shown in blue.

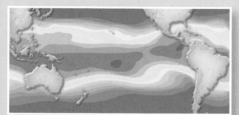

El Niño Warm surface currents flow across the Pacific Ocean to northern South America.

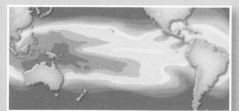

La Niña Warm surface currents flow near Asia and Australia in the western Pacific Ocean.

HEAT

Moving mountain

Days of heavy rain in 2007, brought on by an
El Niño weather pattern, liquefied the soil on
a mountain slope in Peru. Chanchamayo was
in the path of the mudslide. Floodwater rushed
through the village and thick, churning mud
buried houses. Thousands were left homeless.
The force of the raging, debris-filled water
washed away roads and bridges.

Sliding downhill *Sometimes,
steep slopes are unable to
absorb heavy rainfall. When
water-soaked soil liquefies,
gravity pulls the thick mud
downhill. Mudslides can
travel up to 100 kilometres
per hour (60 mph).*

WIND

WATER

HEAT

Munich
Hailstorm

Hail is precipitation that freezes around frozen rain or snow at high altitude in thunderstorm clouds. The biggest hailstones form in long-lived, supercell thunderstorms. Strong updraughts, more than 160 kilometres per hour (100 mph), are needed to repeatedly lift hail within the cloud, allowing layers of ice to build up. Although hail rarely kills people, baseball-sized hail in northern India reportedly killed 250 people in 1888. Hail can strip leaves from trees, destroy fields of crops and kill farm animals.

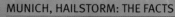

MUNICH, HAILSTORM: THE FACTS

STORM LOCATION: Munich, Germany

STORM DATE: 12 July 1984

STORM STRENGTH: Europe's most damaging hailstorm

DEATH TOLL: 0

Cracked glass *Although not springy like tennis balls, hailstones typically bounce when they land on hard surfaces, such as cars or the ground. Large hail dents car bodies and cracks windscreens.*

HOW HAIL IS MADE

Hail forms when strong winds swirl around ice crystals above the freezing level within an intense thundercloud. Falling hail collects water that freezes slowly and remains clear. Rising hail collects water that freezes quickly and appears cloudy because it is filled with air bubbles.

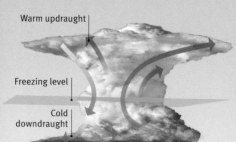

Warm updraught

Freezing level

Cold downdraught

The sky is falling

Hailstones blown by high-speed thunderstorm winds pummelled Munich, Germany, in 1984. Large hail, with a diameter up to 10 centimetres (4 in), fell along a 250-kilometre (155-mi) path, damaging 700,000 houses and 200,000 cars. More than 400 people were wounded. Luckily, nobody was killed. The hailstorm remains the world's second costliest on record.

Cross-section of a hailstone
The interior of a hailstone reveals alternating layers of cloudy and clear ice. At the centre is a small frozen raindrop or snowflake, around which the layers of ice accumulate.

Layers of ice

Frozen raindrop

Damage *Hailstones the size of grapefruit can hit hard enough to penetrate roofs. Smaller, wind-driven hail breaks windows and dents the building's exterior.*

Bubbling under *Strange, bulging formations called mammatus clouds sometimes appear on the underside of thunderclouds. They indicate that powerful updraughts are present within the storm.*

VOLKSWAGEN

WIND

WATER

HEAT

Quebec
Ice Storm

Winter ice storms occur frequently in Canada and parts of the US, Europe and China. These storms form when a shallow layer of freezing, Arctic air is overridden by warm, humid air from lower latitudes. Raindrops fall through the colder air but don't freeze. As soon as these supercooled droplets reach Earth, they freeze solid and can coat everything with thick ice. As the ice accumulates, it weighs down trees. Ice-coated branches don't always break; some bend. Once the ice melts, the trees may return to their original shape or remain bent. If the trunk snaps, the tree will likely die.

QUEBEC, ICE STORM: THE FACTS

STORM LOCATION: Quebec, Canada, and parts of USA

STORM DATE: 4–10 January 1998

STORM STRENGTH: No commonly accepted scale

DEATH TOLL: 35

Winter disaster

In January 1998, freezing rain covered parts of Quebec, Ontario and New England with up to 12.5 centimetres (5 in) of ice. The weight of the ice tore off branches and pulled down power lines. More than 3 million people were affected by power outages, some for longer than a month. Car accidents and hypothermia were responsible for 35 deaths.

Encased in ice *Supercooled raindrops that spread out before freezing form a clear, smooth coating called glaze. When rain slides along an already icy branch, some of the excess water can drip down before freezing. This creates icicles.*

Frozen spray
High winds near large bodies of water can create huge waves. If air near the ground is below freezing, spray from these waves can land on cars, roads and trees, coating them in solid ice.

Crashed car *Even a thin coating of ice can reduce traction, the grip of tyres on a road. Crashes and collisions occur frequently during winter storms.*

Sparks flying *Downed power lines can start fires. Extinguishing fires in ice storm conditions presents serious challenges for firefighters: equipment may become encrusted with ice and water pressure drops significantly when pipes burst.*

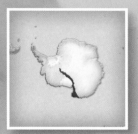

ANTARCTICA, BLIZZARD: THE FACTS

STORM LOCATION: Transantarctic Mountains, Antarctica

STORM SEASON: June–August

STORM STRENGTH: Category 2 hurricane-strength wind

DEATH TOLL: Unknown

Antarctica

Blizzard Alley

A snowstorm with winds stronger than 57 kilometres per hour (35 mph) is called a blizzard. During a "white-out", snow may reduce visibility to less than a metre (3.3 ft). People caught outside can become disorientated as their body temperature drops rapidly. Blizzards are common in the polar regions and on high mountains. In Antarctica, an area near McMurdo Sound at the base of the Transantarctic Mountains has been nicknamed "blizzard alley". Hurricane-strength blizzards, with winds up to 160 kilometres per hour (100 mph), rage there for weeks at a time throughout the year.

Safety in numbers

A colony of male emperor penguins—the only kind of penguin that remains in Antarctica throughout winter—huddle together to survive a ferocious blizzard. Periodically, they shuffle around to get a well-protected inner position, where the temperature can be 20°C (35°F) warmer than the frigid outside air. Average Antarctic temperature is –60°C (–76°F).

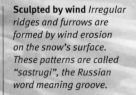

SURVIVING THE COLD

Animals cope with extremely cold conditions by finding shelter, hibernating in winter, storing food internally and working together.

Frozen core *More than a third of the North American wood frog's body freezes in winter. Its heart resumes when warm weather returns.*

Arctic chill *Dense fur, layers of fat and padded feet insulate polar bears from their harsh environment.*

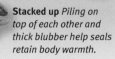

Stacked up *Piling on top of each other and thick blubber help seals retain body warmth.*

Sculpted by wind *Irregular ridges and furrows are formed by wind erosion on the snow's surface. These patterns are called "sastrugi", the Russian word meaning groove.*

WIND

WATER

HEAT

Katabatic winds *Intense winds develop when cold air, which is denser than warm air, flows downhill from mountains and high plateaus. Speed increases as the winds channel through narrow canyons.*

Fluffy down

Layers of feathers

Oily tips

Feathers *A penguin's wings are covered by a dense layer of short, stiff feathers. Fluffy down at the feather base traps warm air, while oily feather tips keep seawater out.*

Fatherly love *Male emperor penguins balance a single egg or newly hatched chick on their feet. If the chick falls to the ground, it can freeze to death in two minutes. While the females hunt for food at sea, the males stand for about two months, through cruel winds and icy temperatures.*

HEAT

WATER

WIND

Austria

Avalanche

An avalanche is a large mass of snow that travels down a mountain. Most avalanches require three ingredients: an unstable snowpack; a steep slope; and a "trigger" to start it. Accumulated snow may start sliding when it can no longer support its own weight or if the base snow slips. Even a small vibration or the motion of a skier can cause snow to break loose. As a precaution, officials frequently set off controlled explosions to produce an avalanche before compacted snow becomes too unreliable. Approximately 150 people die in avalanches around the world each year.

AUSTRIA, AVALANCHE: THE FACTS

EVENT LOCATION: Galtur, Austria

EVENT DATE: 23 February 1999

EVENT STRENGTH: No commonly accepted scale

DEATH TOLL: 31

Crashing down

It took less than a minute for an avalanche to thunder downhill and smash into the town of Galtur, Austria. On impact, the avalanche was 90 metres (300 ft) deep and contained nearly 170,000 tonnes (190,000 t) of snow. Although people had been warned about the danger of potential avalanches, skiers may have actually triggered the catastrophe.

SLIPPERY WHEN WET

Avalanches often happen when new snowfall builds up on top of old, wet or icy snow. Each kind of avalanche is related to temperature, the state of the snowpack and the angle of the slope.

Powder On very steep terrain, snow releases at a point. The avalanche gradually widens as it slides down the slope and forms a teardrop shape.

Slab When a stiff layer of snow fractures, it may dislodge a large block of snow, which crashes down immediately. This often occurs if the base is wet.

Breaking point *Overhanging masses of compacted snow, known as cornices, are prime locations for snowpack fractures.*

Gaining speed *Avalanches accelerate downhill and pick up more snow. Skiing towards the edges of an avalanche may lessen the risk of being buried.*

Dangerous cloud *Some snow usually mixes with air and becomes airborne. A powder cloud, which may be hundreds of metres high, moves faster than the rest of the avalanche. The resulting shock wave can be very destructive.*

Run for cover *Travelling almost 300 kilometres per hour (185 mph), the avalanche breached Galtur's "safety zone", destroyed sturdy buildings and buried 57 people.*

Trapped in snow
People buried by an avalanche can survive for only a short time under the snow. Those trapped in buildings and cars are more likely to live longer. Rescuers use sniffer dogs, probe with long rods, search from the air or simply dig by hand to locate survivors.

Ethiopia
Killer Drought

Droughts are lengthy periods, sometimes many years, with less-than-expected rainfall. They often happen in regions that have marginal rainfall, such as grassland areas next to deserts. Some parts of the world, especially near the Equator, experience recurring droughts every few years. Crops can wither and die without rain or artificial watering systems. When drought, poor farming practices and overpopulation combine, food and water supplies disappear quickly, which can lead to devastating famine. During extended droughts, the environment may suffer irreparable damage. Widespread erosion can result from loss of plant cover and fertile topsoil.

ETHIOPIA, DROUGHT: THE FACTS

EVENT LOCATION: Ethiopia and parts of eastern Africa

EVENT DURATION: 1984–1988

EVENT STRENGTH: No commonly accepted scale

DEATH TOLL: More than one million

All dried up *Lack of rainfall lowers groundwater and lake levels. Small streams are easily affected when sunlight evaporates the remaining water.*

Dying crops *Plants limit water loss by wilting their leaves. The roots may still be alive underground even if the plant looks dead.*

DESERTIFICATION

Extended dry periods combined with poor land management can lead to desertification, when fertile land turns to desert. About one-quarter of Earth's surface is now at risk of becoming desert.

Advancing desert China has lost 93,000 square kilometres (36,000 sq mi) of land to desert since the 1950s. The Chinese government now has a replanting project to hold back the Gobi desert.

WIND

WATER

HEAT

Search for water

Ethiopia and other parts of Africa suffered a disastrous drought from 1984 to 1988. More than 8 million people abandoned their homes to find food and water. Livestock, such as cows, starved and died of thirst and native animals lost their habitat.

Dust devil *Rapidly rising air currents form when the ground is super-heated by the Sun. These updraughts carry dust into the air and create spinning dust devils.*

Cracked earth *Water-starved soil hardens in the Sun and contracts. Moisture can still be present under the surface, but the ground may be too hard to absorb water when it rains and most will run off.*

CANBERRA, FIRESTORM: THE FACTS

STORM LOCATION: Canberra, Australia

STORM DATE: 18–19 January 2003

STORM STRENGTH: 2nd worst fire in Australian history

DEATH TOLL: 4

Canberra

Firestorm

Forest fires are frequently caused by "dry lightning" from thunderstorms that produce little or no rain. People also start fires by accident and sometimes on purpose. Fires spread rapidly up slopes and when strong winds are forced through narrow spaces. If not controlled quickly, small fires can soon become raging infernos. Fires are fuelled by plants and trees, which release flammable chemicals when they burn, starting a chain reaction. A firestorm's intense heat and rising air currents make its own local weather system. Wind gusts may shift a fire's direction and cause the flames to advance faster than a person can run. Fires stop when they run out of fuel and oxygen, if air humidity increases significantly or if it rains.

Fighting fire

Lightning strikes started a fire in a remote national park near Australia's capital, Canberra, in 2003. Hot, dry winds blowing more than 65 kilometres per hour (40 mph) fanned the flames. More than 500 homes and an observatory were destroyed. Firefighters battled against heat, smoke and ash to contain the blaze.

Ember attack *Rising air and strong winds carry burning particles away from the fire's source. A dense, fast-moving concentration of embers can set a car or building ablaze, even when made with special fire-resistant material.*

Twisting fire *Extremely high temperatures in a fire may create rotating winds called a pyronado. This fiery funnel behaves like a small tornado. These flaming updraughts feed themselves and can reach high into the sky.*

Help from above
Aircraft and helicopters "bomb" fires with water or chemicals to lower fire temperatures and make trees less likely to burn.

WIND

WATER

HEAT

SINGAPORE: THE FACTS

STORM LOCATION: Republic of Singapore

STORM SEASON: Greatest activity April–May and November

STORM FREQUENCY: 171 thunderstorm days per year

DEATH TOLL: Unknown

Singapore
Flash Hits

Satellites detect approximately 1.4 billion lightning flashes around the world each year. Most occur over tropical regions near the Equator. There are significantly fewer lightning strikes over oceans. Singapore, a group of islands at the southern tip of the Malay Peninsula, has the second-highest lightning strike rate in the world. Lightning-producing thunderstorms roll through this tiny country an average of 171 days per year, nearly every other day. In peak season, there are 20 lightning days per month. Only the Democratic Republic of Congo in Africa has a higher frequency of lightning strikes.

Prepared for the strike

Singapore takes lightning seriously. Many buildings have conductor rods and surge protection built into their wiring system. Most electrical cables and phone lines are buried underground. Even with these precautions, several people are killed or injured each year. A typical lightning flash discharges about 100 million volts of electricity and creates a massive increase in temperature.

Safe flying *Helicopters and aeroplanes are resistant to the effects of lightning. If struck, the charge flows along the skin of the craft and back out into the air.*

❶

1 **Conductors** Metal rods are placed on top of tall buildings to minimise lightning damage. Cables attached to the rod direct the electricity down to the ground, where it discharges harmlessly.

2 **Protecting nature** More than 120 ancient trees in Singapore's Botanic Gardens have copper cables running along the trunks. If lightning strikes a tree, the flow of electricity runs down the cable and is safely grounded.

3 **Wet strike** When lightning hits a body of water, the charge spreads out across the surface. People have been struck in the water, but many more casualties occur on beaches.

Extreme Weather Events

A weather station must have 10 years' worth of measurements before an extreme reading is deemed an official record.

RECORD-BREAKING WEATHER

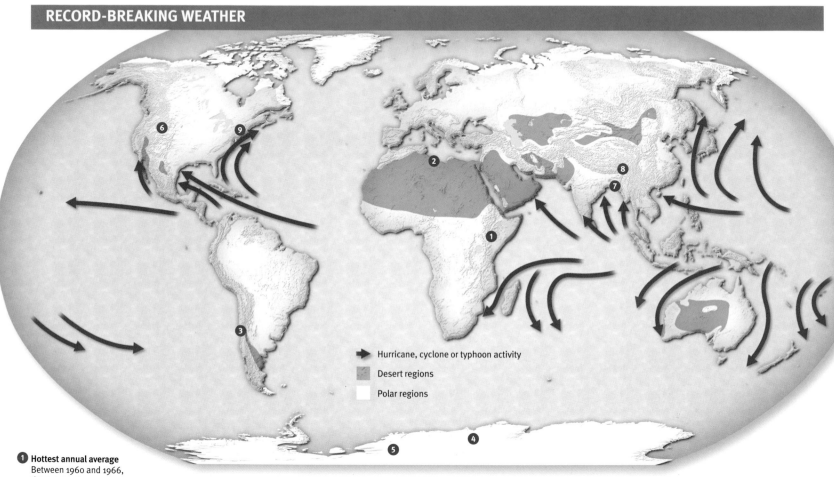

→ Hurricane, cyclone or typhoon activity

■ Desert regions

□ Polar regions

❶ Hottest annual average
Between 1960 and 1966, the average temperature in Dallol, Ethiopia, was 34.4°C (94°F).

❷ Hottest location
In September 1922, Al' Aziziyah, Libya, reached 57.8°C (136°F).

❸ Driest location
The Atacama Desert in Chile has virtually no rainfall. Its average annual rainfall is 0.08 millimetre (0.003 in).

❹ Coldest location
Temperature at Vostok station, Antartica dropped to −89.2°C (−128.6°F) in July 1983.

❺ Coldest annual average
At Pole of Inaccessibility, Antarctica, the average temperature is −58°C (−72°F).

❻ Greatest 24-hour temperature change
The temperature dropped from 6.7°C (44°F) to −49°C (−56°F), in January 1916, in Browning, Montana, USA.

❼ Largest hailstone
In April 1986, a hailstone weighing 1 kilogram (2.25 lb) landed in Gopalganj district, Bangladesh.

❽ Highest annual average rainfall
11,874 millimetres (467 in) at Mawsynram, India.

❾ Highest surface winds
In 1934, 372 kilometres per hour (231 mph) winds were recorded on Mt Washington, New Hampshire, USA.

LIGHTNING STRIKES WORLDWIDE

The Democratic Republic of Congo holds the record for the highest annual rate of lightning strikes. Singapore has the second-highest rate. Colombia, the Himalayas and Florida, USA, are also lightning hot spots. The regions with the most lightning activity are shown in purple (most strikes), red and orange.

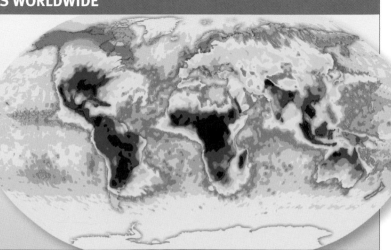

WIND, WATER AND OCEAN WAVES

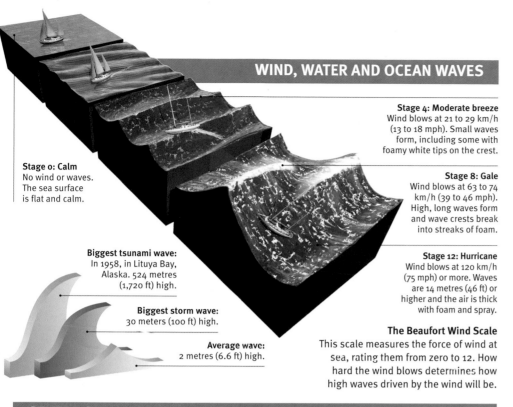

Stage 0: Calm
No wind or waves. The sea surface is flat and calm.

Stage 4: Moderate breeze
Wind blows at 21 to 29 km/h (13 to 18 mph). Small waves form, including some with foamy white tips on the crest.

Stage 8: Gale
Wind blows at 63 to 74 km/h (39 to 46 mph). High, long waves form and wave crests break into streaks of foam.

Stage 12: Hurricane
Wind blows at 120 km/h (75 mph) or more. Waves are 14 metres (46 ft) or higher and the air is thick with foam and spray.

Biggest tsunami wave:
In 1958, in Lituya Bay, Alaska. 524 metres (1,720 ft) high.

Biggest storm wave:
30 meters (100 ft) high.

Average wave:
2 metres (6.6 ft) high.

The Beaufort Wind Scale
This scale measures the force of wind at sea, rating them from zero to 12. How hard the wind blows determines how high waves driven by the wind will be.

SEVERE STORM SAFETY TIPS

Hurricane
In a building •Stay in a secure room away from windows •Unplug electrical appliances •Try to get to the upper levels of a building to escape possible flooding **Outside** •Get inside **In a vehicle** •Drive away from flood-prone areas

Lightning
In a building •Stay inside •Close windows •Unplug electrical appliances **Outside** •Seek shelter in a building •Avoid tall objects •Crouch down in a safe place •Avoid metal **In a vehicle** •Close windows and doors •Do not park under trees

Tornado
In a building •Stay inside far away from windows **Outside** •If there is no safe building, lie flat in a low area •Keep the head covered **In a vehicle** •Do not stay in a vehicle •Do not try to outrun a tornado by driving

Flooding
In a building •Avoid low-lying buildings •Move to the highest area possible **Outside** •Seek shelter in a high place •Avoid rivers, streams and storm drains **In a vehicle** •If caught in rising waters, abandon vehicle and get to high ground

HURRICANES: SAFFIR-SIMPSON SCALE

	WIND SPEED (KM/H) (MPH)	DAMAGE
1	118–152 (74–95)	minimal
2	153–176 (96–110)	moderate
3	177–208 (111–130)	extensive
4	209–248 (131–155)	extreme
5	more than 248 (155)	catastrophic

The Saffir-Simpson scale has been used since the 1970s to classify the severity of hurricanes. The scale is broken into five levels, categorised by the intensity of sustained hurricane-force winds.

TORNADOES: ENHANCED FUJITA SCALE

	SPEEDS (KM/H) (MPH)	DAMAGE
EF0	105–137 (65–85)	light
EF1	138–177 (86–110)	moderate
EF2	178–217 (111–135)	considerable
EF3	218–266 (136–165)	terrible
EF4	267–322 (166–200)	severe
EF5	more than 322 (200)	devastating

The Enhanced Fujita scale rates the strength of a tornado in six categories. Tornadoes in the most extreme category, EF5, are rare.

OCEAN CURRENTS

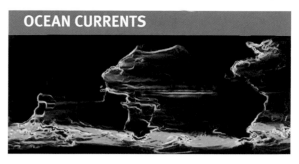

Data about the oceans, including currents and temperature, are used to predict weather patterns. This map shows an Antarctic current running across the bottom. The red and yellow areas are fast-flowing water, while the blue areas are slower currents.

CLOUD TYPES

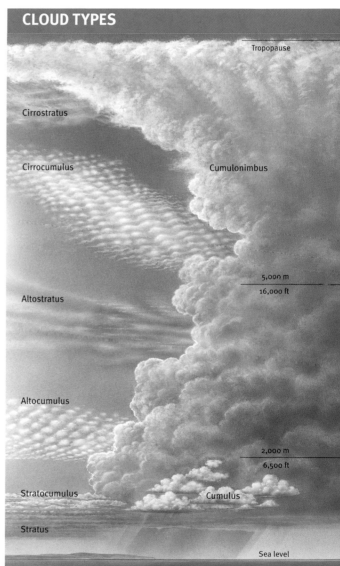

Tropopause

Cirrostratus

Cirrocumulus

Cumulonimbus

Altostratus

5,000 m
16,000 ft

Altocumulus

2,000 m
6,500 ft

Stratocumulus

Cumulus

Stratus

Sea level

Clouds can form at any height, from just above sea level to the top of the troposphere. Clouds are named according to their height and shape by combining the prefixes alto- and cirro- with the Latin words stratus (flat) and cumulus (puffy). Low-level clouds have no prefix.

Glossary

adaptation The way animal species and other living things adjust their features and behaviour to survive.

altitude Height above sea level.

anemometer A device that measures wind speed.

atmosphere Layers of gases that surround a planet, such as Earth.

atmospheric pressure The weight of air above a point on Earth's surface.

aurora A spectacular display of colours that occurs when electrically charged particles generated by the Sun strike oxygen and nitrogen molecules in Earth's atmosphere. Auroras are usually confined to polar regions.

avalanche A large mass of snow that quickly slides down a mountain.

axis An imaginary line through a planet about which it rotates.

barometer An instrument that measures atmospheric pressure.

Beaufort scale A scale devised by William Beaufort in 1805 and used to estimate wind speeds.

blizzard A severe snow storm with winds stronger than 57 kilometres per hour (35 mph).

carbon dioxide A gas in the atmosphere released as living organisms live, die and rot, and by burning fossil fuels, such as oil and coal.

Celsius Scale of temperature in which the melting point of ice is 0° and the boiling point of water is 100°.

cirrus cloud A high, wispy cloud of ice crystals.

climate The weather that occurs in a region over a long period of time.

cloud A visible mass of water droplets and ice suspended in the atmosphere.

cold front The leading edge of a mass of approaching cold air.

condensation The formation of liquid water from water vapour.

convection The upwards and downwards motion of air or water.

Coriolis force The deflection of wind patterns caused by Earth's rotation.

cumulonimbus cloud A large, tall cumulus cloud that produces thunder and lightning.

cumulus cloud Puffy, white, low cloud.

current The flow of air, water or electricity.

dam A barrier blocking the flow of water, air or other material.

desert An area that receives little rain and has little, if any, vegetation.

desertification The process by which fertile land turns into desert.

downdraught A downward-moving air current.

dropsonde An instrument-filled canister dropped from an aircraft into a tropical storm to capture scientific information about the storm.

drought An extended period with little or no rain.

dust devil A small, upward-spiralling whirlwind containing dust or sand.

El Niño An unusually warm sea current off the western coast of South America that arrives every two to seven years. El Niño cycles often alternate with La Niña cycles that bring an unusually cold sea current off the western coast of South America.

Equator An imaginary line that lies halfway between the North and South poles.

evaporation The process by which water turns into water vapour.

eye The clear area in the centre of a hurricane.

Fahrenheit Scale of temperature in which the melting point of ice is 32° and the boiling point of water is 212°.

firestorm A large, incredibly hot fire that creates its own localised weather system.

flash flood A sudden rise of fast-flowing water.

flood A long-term rise in river and stream levels in which lands nearby become covered with water.

fog Cloud that forms near or on the ground.

frost An icy coating that forms when moisture in the air freezes onto grass, glass and other things.

glacier A body of ice, formed from compressed, accumulated snowfall, that moves slowly down a valley or slope.

global warming An increase in the average temperature of Earth's atmosphere.

Gulf Stream An ocean current that carries warm water from the Caribbean Sea to the North Atlantic Ocean.